THE
FISHERMAN'S
GUIDE TO
LIFE

*Timely Tips and Timeless Wisdom
about Fishing and Life*

The quoted ideas expressed in this book (but not Scripture verses) are not, in all cases, exact quotations, as some have been edited for clarity and brevity. In all cases, the author has attempted to maintain the speaker's original intent. In some cases, quoted material for this book was obtained from secondary sources, primarily print media. While every effort was made to ensure the accuracy of these sources, the accuracy cannot be guaranteed. For additions, deletions, corrections, or clarifications in future editions of this text, please write Freeman-Smith, LLC.

The Holy Bible, King James Version (KJV)

The Holy Bible, New International Version (NIV) Copyright © 1973, 1978, 1984, by International Bible Society. Used by permission of Zondervan Publishing House. All rights reserved.

The Holy Bible, New King James Version (NKJV) Copyright © 1982 by Thomas Nelson, Inc. Used by permission.

The Holman Christian Standard Bible™ (HCSB) Copyright © 1999, 2000, 2001 by Holman Bible Publishers. Used by permission.

Cover Design by Kim Russell / Wahoo Designs
Page Layout by Bart Dawson

ISBN 978-1-60587-224-7

Printed in the United States of America

THE FISHERMAN'S GUIDE TO LIFE

Timely Tips and Timeless Wisdom about Fishing and Life

Table of Contents

If fishing interferes with
your business,
give up your business.

—

Sparse Grey Hackle

Introduction

Our most profound lessons, first learned in childhood, must be relearned again and again throughout life. We know the fundamental principles all too well: fairness, honesty, optimism, and love, to name a few. But in the wake of the daily grind, we forget. The universal human dilemma is this: Perspective is a perishable commodity.

Fishing restores perspective. When we escape to the solitude of quiet waters, the day's fleeting troubles seem to evaporate into the mist; in the presence of nature, spiritual order is restored.

The observant angler has many lessons to learn, and this book addresses a few of them. Utilizing the words of renowned fishermen, writers, and philosophers, each principle is examined in light of its application to fishing and, more importantly, its application to life.

Whether we visit the neighborhood pond, the bubbling brook, or the open seas, the message of the waters is the same: Be prepared, be patient, and enjoy the moment. Some days the fish will bite; some days they won't. In the grand scheme, the size of a day's catch isn't very important. But whenever we go down to the water and rediscover an important lesson about life—sure enough, that's a keeper.

Lesson 1

Carpe Diem

The Trip Is Brief—Enjoy It

A good fishing trip, like a well-cooked meal or a well-lived life, always ends a little too soon. Time on the water is a priceless gift, a gift that should never be taken for granted.

The wise angler understands that every trip to the water is, in a sense, his last. Because nature is constantly changing, no man fishes the same water twice—even if he spends a lifetime casting into a single small pond. The fish, the water and the weather are in a state of constant flux; more importantly, the angler himself is changing with each passing day.

The German philosopher Goethe wrote, "Every second is of infinite value." And so it is with fishing. The trip is altogether too brief, so why not savor every moment?

*This is the day the LORD has made;
we will rejoice and be glad in it.*

—

Psalm 118:24 NKJV

When is the best season of the year to go a-fishing?
When you feel like it and can
leave home and business.

Charles Bradford

The two best times to go fishing are
when it's raining and when it's not.

Fisherman's Saying

Fishing seems to be the favorite form of loafing.

Ed Howe

No life is so happy and so pleasant
as the life of
the well-govern'd angler.

—

Izaak Walton

Angling is the way to round out a happy life.

Charles K. Fox

If you wish to be happy for eight days,
kill your pig and eat it.
If you wish to be happy for a lifetime, learn to fish.

Chinese Proverb

One thing becomes clearer as one gets older and
one's fishing experience increases,
and that is the paramount importance
of one's fishing companions.

John Ashley-Cooper

I now believe that fishing is far more important than the fish.

—

Arnold H. Glasgow

I have fished through fishless days that I remember
happily and without regret.

Roderick Haig-Brown

Every intelligent sportsman knows that
the greatest rewards of hunting
and fishing are irresistible.

Ted Trueblood

Why do people go fishing?
Some say they fish to get fish.
This is obviously false.

John W. Randolph

'Tis not all of fishing to fish.

Izaak Walton

For the true angler, fishing produces a deep,
unspoken joy, born of longing for that which is
quiet and peaceful, and fostered by
an inbred love of nature.

Thaddeus Norris

Fishing is the chance to wash one's soul with
pure air, with the rush of the brook,
or with the shimmer of the sun on blue water.

Herbert Hoover

I have experienced such simple joy in the trivial
matters of fishing and sport formerly as might
inspire the muse of Homer or Shakespeare.

Henry David Thoreau

Angling is somewhat like poetry.

Izaak Walton

A bad day fishing still beats
a good day working.

—

Fisherman's Saying

The angler is never a has-been.
He enjoys a lifetime of participation which
continues through noon, then on into the sunset,
and even into the eventide of life.

Charles K. Fox

He who is contented is rich.

Lao Tzu

Happiness is not a state to arrive at,
but a manner of traveling.

Samuel Johnson

Of all the world's enjoyments,
That ever valued were;
There's none of our employments
With fishing can compare.

Thomas D'Urfey

No fisherman ever fishes
as much as he wants to.

Geoffrey Norman

Fish come and go, but it is the memory
of afternoons on the stream that endure.

E. Donnall Thomas

*Then God saw everything
that He had made,
and indeed it was very good.*

—

Genesis 1:31 NKJV

When you're fishing,
you're in an ancient world
that changes very little,
even over centuries.

—

Arthur Cone, Jr.

You didn't know the day was half over and all
of a sudden you have an acute sense of how brief
a day is. You are not thinking of yourself so much
as the day and everything in it — the river, the life
around you, even the sound and odor of things.
Being in the river all day has put you inside of its
sinuous, convoluted time, and suddenly you feel
you have shared the day, and lost it,
with everything around you.

Christopher Camuto

One of my favorite aspects of each trip
was telling Mama and my sisters about
my part for a few days in a man's world.
I proudly described our experiences,
most of them not needing much enhancing
to make them interesting.

Jimmy Carter

We live day to day with little
change in our perceptions,
but I never go to a river that
I do not see newly and freshly,
that I do not learn.

—

Nick Lyons

There is only one thing wrong
with a fishing day—
its staggering brevity.
If a man spent all his days fishing,
life would seem to be
a swift dream.

—

Zane Grey

If a man fishes hard, what is he going to do easy?

Roy Blount, Jr.

Ignorant men don't know what good they hold
in their hands until they've flung it away.

Sophocles

Time deals gently only with those
who take it gently.

Anatole France

It is now and in this world that we must live.

André Gide

After all these years,
I still feel like a boy
when I'm on a stream or lake.

—

Jimmy Carter

Angling is not only
a most agreeable and delightful
amusement—
it also imparts health and long life.

—

Palmer Hackle, Esq.

Those rivers and their bounty—
bright and wild—
touch me and through me touch
every person whom I meet.

—

Nick Lyons

The trout do not rise
in the cemetery,
so you better do your fishing
while you are still able.

—

Sparse Grey Hackle

Lesson 2

Lifetime Learning

The Ultimate Lure
Is the Mind of the Fisherman

I n the days before hooks, lines, rods, and reels, a fisherman relied on creativity for his daily catch. His tackle consisted of such unlikely items as sticks, spears, animal parts, even spider webs. And he caught fish.

Today, quality tackle is available to every angler whose income is sufficient to support his habit. But the most important lure remains the knowledge and ingenuity of the fisherman.

For the uninitiated, catching fish is a simple business: bait a hook; drop it in the water; see what happens. The seasoned angler knows better. Fish are not so much caught as they are out-smarted.

Some fishermen, through a commitment to lifetime learning, transform sport into art. The following quotations celebrate those anglers who, like their prey, never stop schooling.

*Happy is the man who finds wisdom,
and the man who gains understanding.*

—

Proverbs 3:13 NKJV

No man ever became wise by chance.

Seneca

No one is born an artist nor an angler.

Izaak Walton

The wisest mind has something yet to learn.

George Santayana

Books can't make you a good fisherman,
but they can make you a better one.

Fisherman's Saying

A man should never stop learning,
even on his last day.

Maimonides

He knows enough who knows how to learn.

Henry Adams

To be a good angler, one must have
a good knowledge of fish, for to understand
the quarry is to defeat him.

Tiny Bennett

All veteran anglers have their tricks of the trade.
Usually you have to fish a long time
to pick them up.

Wheeler Johnson

It's what you know after
you know it all that counts.

Harry S Truman

All things are difficult before they are easy.

Thomas Fuller

Anglers are not born, they are made by
circumstances, and sometimes it takes a long time
to get the right circumstances together.

John W. Randolph

Casting is not the end of knowledge.
In fact it is only the beginning.

Geoffrey Norman

I am still learning.

Michelangelo's Motto

The years have much to teach which
the days never know.

Ralph Waldo Emerson

Learning to catch fish is not difficult,
but becoming a reasonable expert at it
does require time and study.

—A. J. McClane

Nature is always hinting at us.

Robert Frost

The great charm of fly fishing
is that we are always learning.

Theodore Gordon

One of the charms of the sport is its infinite
complexity. The wood has enough depth and
richness to reward a lifetime of quiet,
perspective searching.

Roderick Haig-Brown

A man, though wise,
should never be ashamed of learning more.

Sophocles

Wisdom is the principal thing; therefore get wisdom.
And in all your getting, get understanding.

Proverbs 4:7 NKJV

Education is hanging on until you've caught on.

Robert Frost

Anyone who stops learning is old,
whether at twenty or eighty.

Henry Ford

A whale ship was my Yale and my Harvard.

Herman Melville

Angling may be said to be
like mathematics in that
it can never fully be learnt.

—

Izaak Walton

You cannot step twice
in the same river,
for other waters are continually
flowing on.

—

Heraclitus

Beyond every bend in a stream lies
a new fishing challenge,
for no pool or rapids is just like
the previous one.

—

Dick Sternberg

Every lesson you learn,
no matter where you learn it,
transfers to all other rivers,
no matter where you fish.

—

Dave Hughes

Successful anglers are sticklers for doing everything
precisely right, because they know a slight
difference in technique can make
a big difference in the catch.

Ted Trueblood

Successful hunters and fishermen are precise
observers of the world around them.
They have to be in order to be successful.

George Reiger

Every man who observes vigilantly and resolves
steadfastly grows unconsciously into genius.

Edward Bulwer-Lytton

You can observe a lot just by watching.

Yogi Berra

A man that goeth to the river for
his pleasure must understand
the Sun, and the Wind, the
Moon, and the Stars, and set forth
his tackle accordingly.

—

Thomas Barker

Nothing is ever simple about fish,
whether it's catching them
or understanding them.

A. J. McClane

Knowledge comes but wisdom lingers.

Alfred, Lord Tennyson

The skill to do comes from doing.

Ralph Waldo Emerson

If you take your boat into the shallow waters,
you had better know where the stumps are.

Fisherman's Saying

A fishing notebook is invaluable,
and all serious anglers
should keep one.

—

Ted Trueblood

Your headiest success as an angler begins
when you start caring more about
fishing than the fish.

Arnold Gingrich

Man can learn a lot from fishing.
When the fish are biting, no problem in the world
is big enough to be remembered.

O. A. Battista

Four-fifths of the earth's surface
is covered with water,
but only five percent of that is good fishing.

Geoffrey Norman

The secret of successful angling depends on
learning the kind of water the fish prefer,
and then concentrating on it.

Ted Trueblood

Most of the world is covered
with water.
A fisherman's job is simple:
Pick out the right parts.

—

Charles F. Waterman

The best fisherman in the world
can't catch them if they aren't there.

Anthony Acerrano

When there are no fish in one spot,
cast your hook in another.

Chinese Proverb

The wary angler in the winding brook knows
the fish and where to bait his hook.

Ovid

All devotees of nature and the outdoors are
prophets and promulgators of a kind of gospel.
They are the communicants of a common faith.

Alan Devoe

The personality of a river is not to be found in
its water, nor its shape. The life of a river, like that
of a human being, consists in the union of soul
and body, the water and the banks.

Henry Van Dyke

Never, no never, did Nature say one thing,
and wisdom another.

Edumond Burke

The river has taught me to listen; you will learn
from it, too. The river knows everything; one can
learn everything from it. You have already learned
from the river that it is good to strive downwards,
to sink, to seek the depths.

Herman Hesse

A thousand fishing trips
go by, indistinguishable from
one another, and then
suddenly one comes along that is
fatefully perfect.

—

A. J. McClane

Ten percent of the fishermen catch
ninety percent of the fish.

—

Fisherman's Saying

The hardest part of fishing is learning
to read water.

Geoffrey Norman

You can't learn any stream by heart
in less than three seasons.

Arnold Gingrich

The first principle of reading water is this:
Fish are found at the edges of things.

Charles F. Waterman

Every fishing water has its secrets.
To yield up these mysteries,
it must be fished with more than hooks.

Zane Grey

Anybody can see the weeds.
It takes a little practice to notice
the less obvious features.

Charles F. Waterman

Learn to visualize the lake without the water.

Jim Chapralis

The man who keeps everything locked up
in his heart will know far less than he who
compares notes with his fellows.

Theodore Gordon

Men learn while they teach.

Seneca

I learn from anyone, but I do not stop at that.
I go on trying to learn from myself.

Zane Grey

Give a man a fish and you feed
him for a day.
Teach a man to fish and you feed
him for a lifetime.

—

Ancient Proverb

If you want to catch fish,
you'd better be fishing
in the right pond.

—

Fisherman's Saying

Unless you change how you fish,
you will always catch the same size fish.

Chuck Bauer

Fishing is an educational process that lasts
a lifetime. Its diploma consists of the fish you
catch and the memories you make,
but not necessarily in that order.

Criswell Freeman

Fishing is cumulative,
though you don't learn all of it, ever.

Nick Lyons

I didn't learn to love fishing.
I was born loving fishing.

Bob Becker

A really successful angler
is a person with imagination.

Arthur Cone, Jr.

Time may alter the kind or
quantity of angling we do,
but it never ends our opportunity.

—

George Reiger

Fishing is also a teacher.
The lessons learned in
a fishing boat are not lost when
you return to shore.

—

Ron Schara

In fishing, as in warfare,
being in the right place
at the right time
makes all the difference.

—

Arthur Cone, Jr.

Any man who pits his intelligence
against a fish, and loses,
has it coming.

—

John Steinbeck

Lesson 3

The Tackle Box

The Better the Lure, the Bigger the Fish

Scottish-born author Thomas Carlyle wrote, "Man is a tool-using animal. Without tools he is nothing; with tools, he is all." These words are particularly true as they apply to the art of angling.

The serious fisherman understands that success on the water begins with the acquisitions and organization of a well-stocked tackle box. The fisherman who wishes to improve his catch must first improve his tools. In fishing, as in life, preparation is the better part of luck.

*The plans of the diligent
lead surely to plenty.*

—

Proverbs 21:5 NKJV

Prepare your tackle.
When you hook a big fish,
it is impossible to retie a knot or
change a leader.

—

Jim Chapralis

Organization is a habit.

George Allen

It's the little details that are vital.
Little things make big things happen.

John Wooden

Good people order and arrange.

Confucius

The secret to success in life is for a man
to be ready for his opportunity when it comes.

Benjamin Disraeli

A good fisherman can secure
many regenerative hours in winter,
polishing up the rods and reels.

—

Herbert Hoover

The joys of fishing are not
confined to the hours
near the water.

—

Herbert Hoover

A fisherman will spend almost as much time in the tackle shops as he will upon a trout stream.

—

William Hjortsberg

Handle your tools without mittens;
remember that the cat in gloves catches no mice.

Ben Franklin

Spectacular achievements are always preceded by
unspectacular preparation.

Roger Staubach

The best investment is in
the tools of one's own trade.

Ben Franklin

If you need a piece of equipment and don't buy it,
you pay for it even if you don't have it.

Henry Ford

I have no need for new rods,
for mine, like well-kept violins,
have rather improved by age.

—

Barnet Phillips

Forewarned is forearmed.
To be prepared is half the victory.

Miguel de Cervantes

When opportunity comes, it's too late to prepare.

John Wooden

Luck affects everything; let your hook always be
cast. In the stream where you least expect it,
there will be fish.

Ovid

The angler should try all types of lures
until he discovers just which one will do
the best job that day.

Joe Brooks

The best way
to communicate with a fish
is to drop it a line.

—

Anonymous

One of the turning points of
my life was when I got my first
bait-casting outfit.

—

Jimmy Carter

Your outfit may be elaborate,
or it may be a cane pole.
Fortunately, the size of your kit
is no indication
of the pleasure you derive.

—

Jack Randolph

He that would catch fish must first
venture his bait.

Ben Franklin

You can catch your next fish with
a piece of the last.

Oliver Wendell Holmes

Venture a small fish to catch a great one.

Thomas Fuller

The reason life sometimes
seems dull is because we do not
perceive the importance and
excitement of getting bait.

—

Henry Van Dyke

A dirty-looking lure marred by a year's worth of
abuse or neglect won't produce nearly
as well as a squeaky clean one with hooks
honed to a piercing edge.

Tommy Martin

One of the greatest dangers in fishing
is the danger of succumbing to the temptation
of all the gizmos, do-dads,
and whats-its available to the fisherman.

Joe Panfalone

Why make a simple thing like fishing so difficult?

Arthur Cone, Jr.

Consider building a rod for
yourself.

—

Ian Scott

Thomas Edison spent two years trying to find
one element that would burn and shed light
without burning up and out.
He kept up this unrewarding, trial-and-error activity
with the same fever and persistence successful
fishermen exercise in their never-ending quest
for the "perfect lure."

Paul Quinnett

We know that the true fisherman finds no better
time for profitable contemplation and mental
exercise than when actually engaged
with his angling outfit.

Grover Cleveland

The very first equipment I had was a birch pole.
My dad cut it for me. A piece of wrapping string
and a penny's worth of ring hooks (they were five
for a penny in those days) and a cork from
an old bottle completed the necessary outfit.
Well, they were the good old days. I guess
there's many a grown-up man can look back and
remember birch pole days. And maybe,
he'd be willing to trade even just to
have them back.

Lou J. Eppinger

In these sad and ominous days of mad
fortune-chasing, every patriotic, thoughtful citizen,
whether he fishes or not, should lament
that we have not among our countrymen
more fishermen.

Grover Cleveland

Unless you have a ritual
for getting your tackle box ready,
no one will regard you
as a serious fisherman.

—

John. W. Randolph

If they ain't no fish,
no pole or rod,
or no kind of fancy tackle
will catch them.

—

Lou J. Eppinger

It is a tried and true axiom
that as a fisherman grows more
specialized and refined
in his pursuits, the equipment
he needs becomes increasingly
complex and varied.

—

William Hjortsberg

Tackle box:
a container, of any size,
that is too small
to hold all the lures you need.

—

Criswell Freeman

Lesson 4

Patience

You Can't Hurry a Fish

Nature marches to the beat of its own drum. And fish bite when they're ready, not before. An angler's frustration will not force a fish to bite. Nor will his worry.

Since one can't hurry a fish, angling inevitably becomes a lesson in patience and persistence. Once a fisherman has done his best, the rest must be left up to his prey.

So remember: If the fish aren't biting, let them not bite. But keep fishing. The next cast may hook the big one.

*Patience is better than power,
and controlling one's temper,
than capturing a city.*

—

Proverbs 16:32 HCSB

The greatest fishing secret ever? Patience.

—

Donald Jack Anderson

Patience is the companion of wisdom.

St. Augustine

To do nothing is sometimes a good remedy.

Hippocrates

Patience achieves more than force.

Edmund Burke

Nine-tenths of wisdom is being wise in time.

Theodore Roosevelt

There is a final moment of
unyielding patience which,
in angling, so often makes
the difference between
fish and no fish.

—

Sparse Grey Hackle

Angling is an art worthy
of the knowledge and practice
of a wise man.

—

Izaak Walton

All human power is a compound
of time and patience.

Honoré de Balzac

The greatest and most sublime power is often
simple patience.

Horace Bushnell

Who longest waits most surely wins.

Helen Hunt Jackson

You can't catch fish on a dry line.

Fisherman's Saying

Persistence, for the fisherman,
is a virtue that transcends
patience.

—

A. J. McClane

How poor are they that have not patience!

William Shakespeare

The hasty angler loses the fish.

Fisherman's Saying

All human wisdom is summed up in two words:
wait and hope.

Alexandre Dumas

All you need to be a fisherman is
patience and a worm.

—

Herb Shriver

All things come to those who bait.

—

Fisherman's Saying

So frequent the casts.
So seldom the strikes.

Arnold Gingrich

Be content:
The sea hath fish enough.

Thomas Fuller

Have patience with all things,
but mostly with yourself.

St. Francis de Sales

There is a time to fish and a time to dry the nets.

Fisherman's Saying

There is a rhythm to an angler's life
and a rhythm to his year.

Nick Lyons

The fisherman loves to row out in the stillness of
the mists of the morning when the lake
is like polished black glass.

Ernest Lyons

When the fish decide not to bite,
there's no use trying to convince them otherwise.
Fish operate according to their own timetables,
ignoring the impatient pleas of emotional anglers.
The wise fisherman learns patience
in the face of an empty net.

Criswell Freeman

You have to be prepared to sit all day long
and wait for that big one to bite.

Bob Crupi

Fishing is mostly tough luck.
"The big ones get away" is its basic slogan.
And the bigger the fish an angler seeks,
the tougher his misfortune is likely to be.

Philip Wylie

Whether you fish tournaments
or just enjoy
the occasional weekend trip,
patience is a virtue
when it comes to fishing.

—

Roger Bacon

It is, I think, this unquenchable curiosity that
makes our species unique. It is this wondering,
this insatiable thirst to explore beyond our reach,
that leads us, with nothing more than hook and
line, to reconnoiter where we cannot go and
canvass what we cannot see.

Paul Quinnett

Endurance is nobler than strength,
and patience nobler than beauty.

John Ruskin

And not all the greatness was in the sport, the luck,
the fish itself. It is the spirit that counts.
The boy or man who can be true to an ideal,
stick to a hard task, carry on in the face of failure,
exhaustion, seeming hopelessness—
he is the one who earns the great reward.

Zane Grey

If at first you don't succeed, hang in there!
If you're striking out, change lures and techniques
until you find something that works.
Keep your hook in the water and never give up.

George H. W. Bush

All good abides with him who waits wisely.

Henry David Thoreau

Patience achieves more than force.

Edmund Burke

It is known of all men that
one of the rudiments in
the education of a true fisherman
is the lesson of patience.

—

Grover Cleveland

There is distinct similarity between cattle and
casters in that each regards the grass as being
greener on the other side of the fence.

Charles K. Fox

The best fish swim deep.

Thomas Fuller

Fishing is chancy and mysterious,
and a challenge all the days of a man's life.

Paul Quinnett

I knew an old fisherman who said he enjoyed
the times when the fish weren't biting,
for then he had time to see and hear
all the things he would miss if he were
too busy hauling in fish.

Archibald Rutledge

Only the game fish swims upstream.

John Trotwood Moore

Be patient and calm—
for no one can catch fish in anger.

Herbert Hoover

There's no taking fish in dry breeches.

Miguel de Cervantes

Character is that which can do without success.

Ralph Waldo Emerson

If you want to catch more fish,
use more hooks.

George Allen

If you're in a hurry to catch fish,
you should ask yourself
this question:
"What's the hurry?"

—

Harvey Freeman

A fisherman has many dreams.
Some dreams, even those
of a fisherman, come true.

—

Zane Grey

Adopt the pace of nature; her secret is patience.

—

Ralph Waldo Emerson

A fisherman must be of
contemplative mind,
for it is a long time between bites.

—

Herbert Hoover

Lesson 5

Respect for Nature

Leave the River as You Found It

Zane Grey wrote, "If I fished only to capture fish, my fishing trips would have ended long ago." And so it is with most anglers. The thrill of the catch is often overshadowed by nature's breathtaking grandeur.

Fishermen become a part of the waters they fish. As naturalist John Muir observed, "When one tugs on a single thing in nature, one finds it attached to the rest of the world."

Only when we approach the water with respect do we gain its fullest measure of enjoyment.

In the beginning God created
the heavens and the earth.
The earth was without form,
and void; and darkness was on
the face of the deep.
And the Spirit of God was hovering
over the face of the waters.
Then God said, "Let there be light";
and there was light.

—

Genesis 1:1-3 NKJV

Rivers and the inhabitants
of the watery elements are made
for wise men to contemplate
and for fools to pass by without
consideration.

—

Izaac Walton

It is difficult to talk to people
who are not particularly interested
in the value of a river.

—

Zane Grey

Day's sweetest moments are at dawn.

Ella Wheeler Wilcox

All our Concord waters have two colors at least:
one when viewed at a distance,
and another, more proper, close at hand.

Henry David Thoreau

I am in love with the green earth.

Charles Lamb

I have never been happier, more exhilarated,
at peace, inspired, and aware of the grandeur of
the universe and greatness of God than when
I find myself in a natural setting not much changed
from the way He made it.

Jimmy Carter

Love all God's creation, both the whole and every grain of sand. Love every leaf, every ray of light. Love the animals, love the plants, love each separate thing. If thou love each thing thou will perceive the mystery of God in all.

Feodor Dostoevsky

Nature is an unlimited broadcasting station through which God speaks to us every hour— if we will only tune in.

George Washington Carver

Listen to Nature's teachings.

William Cullen Bryant

Those who dwell, as scientists or laymen, among the beauties and mysteries of the earth are never alone or weary of life.

Rachel Carson

No winter lasts forever,
no spring skips its turn.
April is a promise that
May is bound to keep,
and we know it.

—

Hal Borland

We need the tonic of wildness.
At the same time that we are earnest to explore
and learn all things, we require that all things be
mysterious and unexplorable, that land and sea be
infinitely wild, unsurveyed, and unfathomed by us
because unfathomable. We can never have enough
of nature. We must be refreshed by the sight of
inexhaustible vigor, vast and titanic features.

Henry David Thoreau

For real company and friendship,
there is nothing outside of the animal kingdom
that is comparable to a river.

Henry Van Dyke

Once in a while, spend a week in the woods.
Wash your spirit clean.

John Muir

We would be happy if we studied nature more
in natural things and acted according to nature,
whose rules are few, plain, and most reasonable.

William Penn

Study nature, love nature, stay close to nature.
It will never fail you.

Frank Lloyd Wright

The happiest man is he who learns from
nature the lesson of worship.

Ralph Waldo Emerson

One of the great charms of angling
is that of all the sports,
it affords the best opportunity
to enjoy the wonders
and beauty of nature.

—

J. J. Manley

If you instill in your child
a love of the outdoors and
an appreciation of nature,
you will have given him a treasure
no one can take away.

—

Ted Trueblood

The landscape belongs to the man who looks at it.

Ralph Waldo Emerson

Nature is medicinal and restores their tone.
The tradesman, the attorney, comes out of
the din and craft of the street and sees the sky and
the woods, and is a man again. In their eternal
calm, he finds himself. The health of the eye seems
to demand a horizon. We are never tired,
so long as we can see far enough.

Ralph Waldo Emerson

Fishing is more than fish;
it is the vitalizing lure to outdoor life.

Herbert Hoover

Love of nature
is a common language that can
transcend political and social
boundaries.

—

Jimmy Carter

Flooded with memories and expectations,
we take out our rods, suit up in waders and vest,
special fish hats and nets, arrange flies and lures,
and take to the woods.

Nick Lyons

Nature is painting for us, day after day,
pictures of infinite beauty if only we have
the eyes to see them.

John Ruskin

When I first open my eyes upon the morning
meadows and look out upon the beautiful world,
I thank God I am alive.

Ralph Waldo Emerson

You can't fight nature and win.

Ted Trueblood

Nature will bear the closest inspection.
She invites us to lay our eye level
with her smallest leaf,
and take an insect view of its plain.
Henry David Thoreau

One touch of nature makes the whole world kin.
William Shakespeare

Deviation from Nature is
deviation from happiness.
Samuel Johnson

Let children walk with nature.
John Muir

See Nature, and through her God.

—

Henry David Thoreau

Every river that flows is good
and has something worthy
to be loved.

—

Henry Van Dyke

Perhaps fishing is, for me,
only an excuse to be near rivers.

—

Roderick Haig-Brown

There is always something
wonderful about a new
fishing adventure trip.
Fishing is like Jason's quest
for the Golden Fleece.

—

Zane Grey

When I go fishing, I want to get
away from it all, for it is silence
and solitude even more than it is
fish that I am seeking.
As for big fish, all is relative.
Not every tuna is a trophy.

—

William Humphrey

I have been made to feel more at peace about
my hunting and fishing because of my strict
observance of conservation measures.

Jimmy Carter

The future lies in the strength with which man
can set his powers of creation against
his impulses of destruction.
Perhaps this is the unending frontier.

Marjorie Stoneman Douglas

Many of the most highly publicized events of
my presidency are not nearly as memorable or
significant in my life as fishing with my daddy.

Jimmy Carter

We've earned memories—filled with textures—
that live now in our very marrowbones,
that make us more alive.

Nick Lyons

With appreciation of all
the wonders of nature to be seen,
smelled, or heard on any trip
outdoors, the importance of
the bag grows less.

—

Ted Trueblood

At the outset, the fact should be
recognized that the community of
fishermen constitutes a separate
class or sub-race among
the inhabitants of the earth.

—

Grover Cleveland

When the Creator made all things,
He first made the fishes in the Big Water.

American Indian Legend

A lake is the landscape's most beautiful and
expressive feature. It is the earth's eye,
looking into which the beholder measures
the depth of his own nature.

Henry Van Dyke

I marvel at how the fishes live in the sea.

William Shakespeare

If one really loves nature,
one can find beauty everywhere.

Vincent Van Gogh

Wherever the trout are,
it's beautiful.

—

Thomas Masaryk

The angling fever is a very real
disease and can only be cured
by the application of cold water
and fresh, untainted air.

—

Theodore Gordon

One of the great qualities of fishing is that
it is non-competitive.

John Atherton

To compete against another angler is
to do so once removed and always
on an unequal basis.

Russell Chatham

Fishing is a constant reminder of the democracy
of life, of humility, and of human frailty.
The forces of nature discriminate for no man.

Herbert Hoover

Fishing takes anglers to the best places,
at the best times of year.

Anonymous

A man that goeth to the river for his pleasure
must understand the Sun, and the Wind,
the Moon, and the Stars,
and set forth his tackle accordingly.

Thomas Barker

Successful hunters and fishermen are precise
observers of the world around them.
They have to be in order to be successful.

George Reiger

Eventually all things merge into one and a river
runs through it. The river was cut by the world's
great flood and runs over rocks from the basement
of time. On some rocks are timeless raindrops.
Under the rocks are the words,
and some of the words are theirs.

Norman Maclean

The third chapter of Ecclesiastes reminds us that,
"To every thing there is a season."
For fishermen, each passing season has its own
special beauty and its own special purpose.

Criswell Freeman

Fishing, then, is a sport that provides fun,
food, relaxation, and scenery.

Arthur Cone, Jr.

Along a river in the morning, the world meets you
squarely. My impulse is to watch and listen,
as if I might absorb the frankness that seems to
hover in the air around me. The river slides by,
patient and insistent, as generous
and unforgiving as time.

Christopher Camuto

With rivers, as with good friends, you always feel
better for a few hours in their presence; you always
want to review your dialogue, years later, with
a particular pool or riffle or bend, and to live back
through layers of experience.

Nick Lyons

Fish are not brethren; they are not underlings;
they are other nations, caught with ourselves in
the net of life and time, fellow prisoners
of the splendor and travail of the Earth.

Henry Beston

Nothing in this world so enlivens my spirit and
emotions as the rivers I know.

Nick Lyons

Although we didn't catch as many fish,
the quest was more exciting, as the jack or bass,
using submerged hiding places, obstacles,
and the current to their advantage,
had much more of a fighting chance.

Jimmy Carter

Mountains are good for the ego—
they cut one down to size.

Beatrice Cook

In God's wildness lies
the hope of the world—
the great fresh unblighted,
unredeemed wilderness.
The galling harness of
civilization drops off, and
the wounds heal ere we are aware.

—

John Muir

The angler forgets most of
the fish he catches,
but he does not forget
the streams and lakes in which
they were caught.

—

Charles K. Fox

Every country boy is entitled to a creek.

—

Havilah Babcock

There is certainly something in angling
that tends to produce a serenity of mind.

Washington Irving

Fishing is more than fish.
Fishing is the great occasion when we may return
to the fine simplicity of our forefathers.

Herbert Hoover

If you want fish, fish.

German Proverb

Blessings upon all that hate contention,
and love quietness, and virtue, and Angling.

Izaak Walton

Ultimately, each and every fishing trip begins with
the individual making a single step from
the shore into the water, or from the dock onto
a boat, where he or she hopes and expects the
anxieties of ordinary life to seep away on
the current and tides, allowing him or her to
become someone better.

George Reiger

My advice is go often and visit many localities.
Kill no more fish than you require
for your own eating, and do that in
the most scientific manner.

Charles Bradford

Throw the little ones back.

Fisherman's Saying

Catch no more fish than you can salt.

Fisherman's Saying

Fishing provides that connection
with the whole living world.
It gives you the opportunity of
being totally immersed, turning
back into yourself in a good way.
A form of meditation, some form
of communion with levels of
yourself that are deeper
than the ordinary self.

—

Ted Hughes

It's especially important
that those of us who value
recreation in the outdoors
to be aware of, not only our
impact on the environment, but
also the impact that conservation
programs and legislation have
on the condition of our fish
and their habitat.

—

Arthur Cone, Jr.

A good game is too valuable
to be caught only once.

—

Lee Wulff

The fish is not so much
your quarry as your partner.

—

Arnold Gingrich

Lesson 6

Silence

Quiet Waters Are Wise Counsel

The angler, whether he admits it or not, seeks something more important than his daily limit. He seeks a sense of calm that is as much a part of fishing as hooks and bait. In 1653, Izaak Walton wrote, "God never did make a more calm, quiet, innocent recreation than angling." Even in the relative calm of the 1600s, the joy of fishing stemmed, in part, from man's natural attraction to silence. At its best, angling is a contemplative sport, providing the fisherman with ample opportunity to sort through the fleeting problems of the day.

The most successful fishing trips are not judged by the size of the catch. The lucky angler captures more than fish; he also recaptures a sense of perspective born from the wise counsel of quiet waters.

*In quietness and in confidence
shall be your strength.*

—

Isaiah 30:15 KJV

There is something in fishing
that tends to produce
a gentleness of spirit and
a pure sincerity of mind.

—

Washington Irving

The music of angling is more
compelling to me than anything
contrived in the greatest
symphony hall.

—

A. J. McClane

Nature is a gentle guide.

Minataigne

Never does nature say one thing
and wisdom another.

Juvenal

As civilization, cement pavements,
office buildings and radio have overwhelmed us,
the need for regeneration has increased.
Fishing is a sound, valid reason to go away from
here to somewhere else.

Herbert Hoover

Take rest. A field that has rested gives
a beautiful crop.

Ovid

Fishing is more than a sport.
It is a way of thinking and doing,
a way of reviving the mind
and body.

—

Roderick Haig-Brown

Fishing is not so much getting fish
as it is a state of mind.

—

Herbert Hoover

In its deepest self,
fishing is the most solitary sport,
for at its best it is all between
you and the fish.

—

Arnold Gingrich

Next to prayer,
fishing is the most personal
relationship of man.

—

Herbert Hoover

Silence is the source of great strength.

Lao Tzu

God is the friend of silence.

Mother Teresa

Sometimes, the best use of a mouth is
to keep it closed.

Criswell Freeman

Even a fish stays out of trouble
if he keeps his mouth shut.

Fisherman's Saying

The banks of a river are frequented by a strange
company and are full of mysterious sounds—
the laughter of water, the piping of birds,
the hum of insects and the whispering
of wind in the willows.

Roland Pertwee

We all sprang from common ancestors who lived
their lives in silence that was broken only by
the sounds of nature. Every human being has
an atavistic need for silence.

Ted Trueblood

The best way to fish is alone.

Ellington White

Surely one of the richest bounties of angling is
to grow deeply intimate with the inner life
of the world of nature, and in doing so,
to come closer to your deepest self.

Nick Lyons

By common consent,
fishing is the most peaceful of
all forms of sport.

—H. T. Sheringham

As line spins off the reel of life, the years weave
a crazy pattern. And it is strange how
the seemingly great things become small
and the small things become great.

Ralph Bandini

True silence is the rest
of the mind;
it is to the spirit what sleep
is to the body:
nourishment and refreshment.

—

William Penn

What is empathic in angling is
made so by the long periods
of silences—
the unproductive periods.

—

Thomas McGuane

Many men go fishing
all of their lives without knowing
that it is not fish they are after.

—

Henry David Thoreau

By all means, use some time to be alone.

George Herbert

One of the greatest necessities in America
is to discover creative solitude.

Carl Sandburg

The best thinking has been done in solitude.
The worst has been done in turmoil.

Thomas Edison

Fishing at its most rudimentary level is essentially solitary.

—

Russell Chatham

Fishing:
The solitary and friendly sport.

—

R. Palmer Baker, Jr.

Then come my friend, forget your foes,
and leave your fears behind.
And wander forth to try your luck
with a cheerful, quiet mind.

Henry Van Dyke

It is neither wealth nor splendor,
but tranquility and occupation,
which give happiness.

Thomas Jefferson

On those days when we feel gang hooked ourselves,
and are headed inexorably toward the gaff or
landing net, we need to call upon our wildness to
struggle to break way, to right ourselves,
and to make good our dash to freedom.

Paul Quinnett

Quiet places should be enjoyed.
Save the quiet places first.

Ernest Lyons

Fish quietly. The silence of the wilderness
is too beautiful to miss.

Criswell Freeman

Solitude, particularly for the city man,
is at the heart of fishing for trout.

R. Palmer Baker, Jr.

Time is probably more generous
to the angler than to any other
individual. The wind, the sun,
the open air, the colors and smell,
the loneliness of the sea
or the solitude of the stream,
work for some kind of magic.

—

Zane Grey

Be especially attentive to
noise when fishing in
shallow or clear water.
Keep voices low.

—

Ken Schultz

When it is a long time between bites, and
a fisherman's wits have been dulled by bucolic
scenery, and by quiet sylvan noises at the edge of
perception (such as a million insects chewing
a million blades of grass) and you have lost
the hard focus that comes only from civilization,
then your mind may blither off into vagrant
speculations like these, asking unanswerable
questions, wasting time, making a fool of yourself—
but thank God it is in private, in silence,
where no one else can know what you
are really like and make fun of you!

Keith Gardner

Still water. I rarely fish ponds or lakes,
but a deep, still pool in a mountain stream
is a different kind of stillness,
like the stillness within a heartbeat.

Christopher Camuto

Occasionally a breeze rekindles the fire
and small flames dance silently in the ring of
stones. When the fire rises, I watch the glow of
firelight on birch bark and listen to
the river flow slowly in the dark.

Christopher Camuto

Be still, and know that I am God.

Psalm 46:10 NKJV

There is no peace on earth like that of
being alone in the deep wilderness,
in the glow of a bright campfire.

Charlie Elliott

Someone just back of you
while you are fishing is as bad
as someone looking over your
shoulder while you
write a letter to your girl.

—

Ernest Hemingway

Lesson 7

Humility

You Can't Hook 'Em All

Benjamin Disraeli correctly observed, "There is no education like adversity." Had he been a fisherman, he might have added, "There is no education like an empty catch-net."

Fishing is a humbling sport. Even the most seasoned angler must, from time to time, relearn the lessons that only failure can teach.

Inevitably, we learn more about ourselves in times of trouble than we do in times of plenty. And so it is with fishing. On the following pages, we consider the wisdom of humility as seen through the eyes of the fisherman.

Humility comes before honor.

—

Proverbs 15:33 NIV

Nothing sets a person
so far out of the devil's reach as humility.

Jonathan Edwards

Don't talk too much or too soon.

Bear Bryant

A man wrapped up in himself makes
a very small package.

Ben Franklin

Fisherman's luck means that
the time, the place, the fish,
and you are all together.
It does not happen very often.

—

Zane Grey

No matter how good
a man gets at fishing,
he'll never land every fish
he hooks.

—

A. J. McClane

There was never an angler
who lived but that there was
a fish capable of taking
the conceit out of him.

—

Zane Grey

Bragging may not bring happiness,
but no man having caught a large fish,
goes home through the alley.

Anonymous

The skillful angler must be
full of humble thoughts.

Gervase Markham

It is not a fish until it is on the bank.

Irish Proverb

Pride is surely the most
unbecoming of all vices
in a fisherman.

—

Henry Van Dyke

Thy fate is the common fate of all,
Into each life some rain must fall,
Some days must be dark and dreary.

Henry Wadsworth Longfellow

God resists the proud, but gives grace to the humble.

James 4:6 HCSB

Older anglers know that misfortune is
but a proper contrast to the good days astream.

A. J. McClane

A fish on the hook
is better than ten in the brook.
Fisherman's Saying.

Before honor is humility.
Proverbs 18:12 KJV

It took me five seasons at Catalina
to catch a big tuna.
Zane Grey

He who is content to
"not-catch" fish will have
his time and attention free
for the accumulation of
a thousand experiences.

—

Sparse Grey Hackle

I can't believe one would enjoy
one's kills very much without
a nice percentage of misses.

—

T. H. White

Nothing grows faster
than a fish from the time he bites
until the time he gets away.

—

Fisherman's Saying

Life is a long lesson in humility.

James Barrie

You're in for a great deal of pain
if you take yourself too seriously.

Paul Newman

Going fishing is also a lesson
in humility. Put another way,
to fish is to be humbled—not
once but time and time again.
But that's fine. Such lessons taught
by fish help keep life itself
in perspective.

—

Ron Schara

Don't clean your fish before you catch them.

—

Fisherman's Saying

True humility is contentment.

—

Henri Frédéric Amiel

Lesson 8

Optimism

Cast Hope upon the Waters

Henry Ford once observed, "Whether you think you can or think you can't, you're right." This warning applies to all, but anglers are advised to pay special attention.

Fishing is a sport built upon hope. Each cast is made into uncertain waters, and the final outcome remains in doubt until the quarry is safely in the boat. Some days the fish aren't biting, and no angler on earth can make them rise to the bait. During such times, an optimistic spirit is more valuable than a box full of high-priced tackle.

The pessimist, focusing on his adversity and failures, soon loses hope and retires to the shore. He curses his bad luck, packs up his tackle box, and returns home empty-handed. But the optimistic angler, believing in the inevitability of his success, keeps casting. Eventually the tides turn, and the fish begin to bite.

In fishing, as in life, the size of the catch depends upon the size of one's hopes. On ponds, streams, rivers, lakes, and oceans, the self-fulfilling prophecy is alive and well. And so are the fish.

Hope deferred makes the heart sick.

—

Proverbs 13:12 NKJV

I know of no optimism so great
as that which perennially blooms
in the hearts of the fisherman.

Burton L. Spiller

Great hopes make great men.

Thomas Fuller

Hardships are wonderful for us.
They make us strong.

Lawrence Welk

When things seem hopeless,
keep hoping and get hopping.

Criswell Freeman

Some fishermen see no fish and
foolishly believe
that the river is empty.

—

Henry Van Dyke

Fishermen are an optimistic class,
or they would not be fishermen.

—

Herbert Hoover

Fishing greats, whether they realize it or not, practice PFA: Positive Fishing Approach.

—

Jim Chapralis

Tomorrow will be a new day.
When God sends the dawn, He sends it for all.

Miguel de Cervantes

Wake at dawn with a winged heart
and give thanks for another day.

Khalil Gibran

The message of dawn is hope.

Winston Churchill

Skill is important. Luck and weather
and hope are more important,
and of these, hope is the key.

Paul Quinnett

The biggest mistake most
fishermen make is that they
give up too quickly.
Some days I fish four or five hours
without finding how to catch
the fish, then catch the limit
in the next hour.

—

Ed Todtenbier

How keenly the love of angling is developed in the bosoms of many men; how patient and long suffering fishermen are, and how content with the hope even of small mercies.

—

J. P. Wheeldon

Experience usually is what you get when
you don't get what you want, but if there were
no such thing as optimism, there wouldn't be
any such thing as fishing.

Michael McIntosh

You won't catch every fish you try for,
but don't let that discourage you, because the best
fishermen who every lived can't do it either.

H. G. Tapply

The pessimist sees the difficulty in
every opportunity; the optimist sees
the opportunity in every difficulty.

Lawrence Pearsall Jacks

We are confronted with insurmountable
opportunities.

Walt Kelly

A good angler must bring
a large measure of hope and patience.

Izaak Walton

So many fish, so little time.

Fisherman's Saying

The sun shines not on us, but in us.

John Muir

I'm an optimist,
but an optimist who carries a raincoat.

Harold Wilson

A fisherman is always hopeful—
nearly always more hopeful
than he has any right to be.

—

Roderick Haig-Brown

There are always greater fish
than you have caught,
always the lure of greater task
and achievement, always
the inspiration to seek,
to endure, to find.

—

Zane Grey

Act as if it were impossible to fail.

Dorothea Brande

It is a crime to despair.
We must learn to draw from misfortune
the means of future strength.

Winston Churchill

Nothing is good or bad but thinking makes it so.

William Shakespeare

Every moment of life, I suppose,
is more or less of a turning point.
Opportunities are swarming around us
all the time thicker than gnats at sundown.

Henry Van Dyke

Bait the hook well;
this fish will bite.

—

William Shakespeare

We fishermen dream far more
often of our favorite sport than
other men dream of theirs.

—

Will H. Dilg

Think big. Dream big. Fish big.

—

Anonymous

Fishing makes you think.

Fisherman's Saying

The contentment which fills the mind
of the angler at the close of the day's sport
is one of the chiefest charms in his life.

Rev. William Cowper Prime

You really have to be ready at all times.
Big fish hit when you
least expect it.

Bill Murphy

Even the thousandth trip
to the same old fished-out stream
begins with renewed hope,
with unfailing faith.

—

Zane Grey

Optimism

The fact that reality often stinks
does not deter fishermen.
Remember; the good fisherman travels hopefully.

Paul Quinnett

In the evening, a large pool in a trout stream
represents pure possibility.

Christopher Camuto

The most successful fishermen
are chronically optimistic.

Paul Quinnett

I want a fish to whack the popper
right out of the water, and I hold onto this hope
as long as there is light.

Ellington White

Fishing is hope experienced.

Paul Quinnett

Go forward confidently, energetically attacking
problems, expecting favorable outcomes.

Norman Vincent Peale

Be hopeful!
For tomorrow has never happened before.

Robert Schuller

When asked, "How can you fish all day without
a hit?" the true fisherman replies,
"Hold it! I think I felt something."
When the line again goes slack, he says,
"He'll be back!" This is hope defined.

Paul Quinnett

So long as imagination tempts
and hope persists,
there will remain that
undiscovered star of the angler's
firmament, that biggest fish of all,
the one that got away.

—

Frederick White

Lord, suffer me to catch a fish
so large that even I
in talking of it afterward
shall have no need to lie.

—

Herbert Hoover, Motto at His Fishing Lodge

Lesson 9

Gratitude

Every Day Spent Fishing Is a Day
to Give Thanks

Every day spent fishing should be a day of thanksgiving. Fishermen are surrounded by the beauty of nature, they experience the thrill of the catch, and they enjoy the companionship of fellow anglers. Even when the catch-net is empty, fishing is its own reward.

The following quotations celebrate the joy of angling. These words of wisdom prove once and for all that, in the world of fishing, there are no bad days.

*Thanks be to God for
His indescribable gift.*

—

2 Corinthians 9:15 HCSB

As the angler looks back,
he thinks less of individual
captures and days
than of scenes in which he fished.

—

Lord Grey of Fallondon

The longer I live,
the more beautiful life becomes.

Frank Lloyd Wright

Whether you're an athlete in tip-top physical
condition or a person whose principal exercise is
avoiding exertion, you can find a form
of fishing that will appeal to you.

Arthur Cone, Jr.

Blessings we enjoy daily; and for the most of them,
because they are so common,
most men forget to pay their praise.

Izaak Walton

The true fisherman approaches
the first day of fishing season with
all the sense of wonder and awe of
a child approaching Christmas.

—

Robert Traver

As trauma and change rock
your soul, as you struggle to get
that job to get through college,
no matter where you are,
you can always go fishing for
something.

—

Mark Strand

A trout is a moment of beauty
known only to those
who seek it.

—

Arnold Gingrich

I don't want to sit at the head table anymore.
I want to go fishing.

George H. W. Bush

The proud man counts his newspaper clippings,
the humble man his blessings.

Fulton J. Sheen

We do not see nature with our eyes,
but with our understanding and our hearts.

William Hazlitt

One of the philosophical benefits
of fishing is that it is timeless.
Even if you fish every day—
spring, summer, fall, and winter—
you'll find each one different
from those before and
those that follow.

—

Arthur Cone, Jr.

The first moment
when that float dips is an
experience to be treasured.

—

Conn & Hal Iggulden

Some of the finest moments
I ever had on a fishing trip
happened when I didn't have
the slightest idea where I was,
how I got there, or if I would ever
get back to a trail or a dirt road.

—

Charlie Elliott

Fishing should be the exercise of your skills—
and its rewards the places it brings you to.

Negley Farson

In every fishy place there is magic and mystery—
just waiting to be discovered by
the next angler to come along.

Ron Schara

No duty is more urgent than
that of returning thanks.

St. Ambrose

*Bless the LORD, O my soul,
and forget not all his benefits.*

Psalm 103:2 KJV

Next morning, after a hearty breakfast of mashed potatoes, ham and eggs, and butter from the cream of the cow that browses in the woods, he is off, three miles up the creek, a cigar or his pipe in his mouth, his creel at his side, and his rod over his shoulder, chatting with his chum as he goes; free, joyous, happy; at peace with his Maker, with himself, and all mankind; he should be grateful for this much, even if he catches no fish.

Thaddeus Norris

The poetry of the earth is never dead.

John Keats

How exhilarating the music of the stream!

Thaddeus Norris

Rivers have what man most respects and longs for in his own life and thought—a capacity for renewal and replenishment, continual energy, creativity, cleansing.

John M. Kauffmann

In the course of a lifetime,
fate seems to deal most of us our
full share of earthly blessings.
We get the One Good Dog,
we hook the One Big Fish,
and if we're properly deserving,
we may even find
the One Perfect Partner.

—

H.G. Tapply

God is making the world,
and the show is so grand and
beautiful and exciting that I have
never been able to study any other.

—

John Muir

I come to rivers like
an initiate to holy springs.

—

Nick Lyons

And let's not forget the pure joy of
catching, that moment when
a fishing dream is dancing
on the end of the line.
Memories are made of this.

—

Ron Schara

Perhaps the simple rhythms of life sustained us
through those Great Depression years,
and bass fishing became part of our family rituals.

Ernest Schwiebert

Even today I carry a fish hook and line
tucked away in my pocketbook. It is a habit
brought down from those carefree days when
all the world moved along in a sort of adventurous
charm and expectation.

Charlie Elliott

It's no mystery to us.
Perhaps the only people who are puzzled
by fishing are those who don't do it.

Ron Schara

Even if you never catch anything, lazy afternoons
spent fishing in the summer can be relaxing,
rewarding — and addictive.

Conn & Hal Iggulden

Fishing is timeless and ageless,
and it's a family tradition that should be
passed on to future generations.

Virginia Pierce

In our family, there was no clear line between
religion and fly-fishing.

Norman Maclean

For the truly successful fisherman,
the glass is not half full.
It's filling and about to run over.

—

Paul Quinnett

When you take a family fishing
trip, the best thing to catch
is memories.

—

Anonymous

May your thoughts be always
peaceful, and your heart filled with
gratitude to Him who made
the country and the rivers; and
"may the east wind never blow
when you go-a-fishing!"

—

Thaddeus Norris

The time must come to all of us,
who live long, when memory
is more than prospect.
An angler who reaches this stage
and reviews the pleasure of life
will be grateful and glad
he has been an angler.

—

Lord Grey of Fallondon

Lesson 10

Fishermen Are Funny

Laugh; It's Supposed to Be Fun

On the pages that follow, consider the quirks and absurdities of those who fish. Enjoy.

The fishing was good;
it was the catching that was bad.

—

Fisherman's Saying

Fish stories told here . . .
some true!

—

Fisherman's Saying

I fish; therefore I lie.

—

Fisherman's Saying

There is no greater fan
of fly fishing than the worm.

—

Patrick McManus

A fish is larger for being lost.

Fisherman's Saying

The preposterous luck of a beginner
is well known to all fishermen.
It is an inexplicable thing.

Zane Grey

Work: a dangerous disorder affecting high public
functionaries who want to go fishing.

Ambrose Bierce

"Carpe Diem" does not mean
"fish of the day."

—

Anonymous

Catch and Release:
a conservation strategy that
happens right before game warden
stops your boat.

—

Anonymous

Fishing is not a hobby.
A hobby is something you do in your spare time!

Fisherman's Saying

When the goin' gets tough . . .
the smart go fishin'.

Anonymous

Fishing is a delusion entirely surrounded
by liars in old clothes.

Don Marquis

I fell in love with fishin' hook, line, and sinker . . .
it was love at first bite.

Anonymous

I once gave up fishing.
It was the most terrifying weekend of my life.

Anonymous

I'm great at fishing.
I'm just not too good at catchin'.

Anonymous

There's no known cure for
fishin' fever . . .
except a little more fishin'.

—

Fisherman's Saying

Work is for people
who don't know how to fish.

—

Anonymous

There are two types of
fishermen—
those who fish for sport
and those who fish for fish.

—

Fisherman's Saying

Three-fourths of the Earth's surface is water,
and one-fourth is land. It is quite clear that
the good Lord intended us to spend triple
the amount of time fishing
as taking care of the lawn.

Chuck Clark

What do guides do on their days off?
The best ones go fishing.

Dave Vedder

Why didn't Noah do any fishin' off the Ark?
He only had two worms.

Anonymous

There he stands, draped in more
equipment than a telephone
lineman, trying to outwit
an organism with a brain
no bigger than a breadcrumb,
and getting licked in the process.

—

Paul O'Neil

Catch and Release fishing
is a lot like golf.
You don't have to eat the ball
to have a good time.

—

Anonymous

My rod and my reel,
they comfort me.

—

Fisherman's Saying

Anglers . . . exaggerate grossly and make gentle
and inoffensive creatures sound like
wounded buffalo and man-eating tigers.

Roderick Haig-Brown

Some anglers catch their biggest fish by the tale.

Fisherman's Saying

All fishermen are liars;
it's an occupational disease with them like
housemaid's knee or editor's ulcers.

Beatrice Cook

Time and territory
are the two key factors.
Most people miss the biggest fish
in the lake because
they're fishing at the wrong spot
at the wrong time.

—

Will Kirkpatrick

Calling fly-fishing a hobby is like
calling brain surgery a job.
Paul Schullery

I am not against golf,
since I cannot suspect it keeps armies
of the unworthy from discovering trout.
Paul O'Neil

My biggest worry is that when I'm dead,
my wife will sell all my fishing gear
for what I said I paid for it.
Koos Brandt

Cast carefully, as a hook catching your eyebrow
is a deeply unpleasant experience.

Conn & Hal Iggulden

You will search far to find a fisherman to admit
that a taste for fishing, like a taste for liquor,
must be governed lest it come
to possess its possessor.

Sparse Grey Hackle

How many fathers look at a brand-spanking-new
baby girl and think "fishing buddy"?
Not enough, I can tell you.

Paul Quinnett

It's pure luck that the absence of fish corresponds
to the Christmas season when fishermen-family
acquaintanceship is renewed,
and Father is pleased to see how much
the children have grown since
he last noticed them.

Beatrice Cook

When you are fishing alone,
you had better bring your fish home if you want
your friends and family to believe you.

R. Palmer Baker, Jr.

The fishing isn't what it used to be,
but then, what is?

Arthur Gordon

Sometimes the recollection of our boyish sports
comes back to us after manhood, and one who
has been "addicted" to fishing relapses into his old
"ailment"; then angling becomes a pleasant kind
of disease, and one's friends are apt to become
inoculated with the virus, for it is contagious.

Thaddeus Norris

One of the advantages of worming, we discovered
early on, was that it discouraged little girls from
wanting to go fishing with us. When we got
to be sixteen, however, we learned that it also
discouraged big girls from wanting to go fishing
with us. Most of us switched to flies then, claiming
that worms really weren't a sporting bait.

Patrick F. McManus

Fishermen are born honest, but they get over it.

Ed Zern

If it's a nice day, find a place to sit,
and enjoy the peace that lasts until someone
comes along and says, "Any luck?"

Conn & Hal Iggulden

Many people think fishermen are born liars.
This is not true.
Fishermen acquire the talent.

Paul Quinnett

Old fishermen never die.
They just smell that way.

—

Fisherman's Saying

Lesson 11

Observations on Fishing and Life

On the pages that follow, observe the angling attitude about life and fishing. Enjoy.

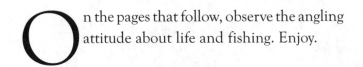

But veterans also know that as we grow older,
fishing becomes as much about ritual and
memory as putting new notches on the reel.

George Reiger

The old man casting over a darkening pool
and the white-haired lady watching her sand-spiked
rod nod to the surf are only variations on
the little boy who once chased suckers
in the shallows or the little girl who collected
shells along the beach.

George Reiger

The mystery of the fishes
is a very big one
and you need several lifetimes to
solve even part of it.

—

Paul Quinnett

If people concentrated
on the really important things
in life, there'd be a shortage of
fishing poles.

—

Doug Larson

Fishermen don't yield to the weather.

Jack MacKinnon

Anglers have a way of romanticizing
their battles with fish.

Ernest Hemingway

Angling has this distinction of its own:
The very poorest man can, if he so chooses,
become a fisherman.

J. P. Wheeldon

Catching a fish can be exciting—the real skill is
not in hooking one, but in bringing it in without
breaking the line or losing the fish.

Conn & Hal Iggulden

I have never yet caught a fish on a first cast,
nor have I never made a first cast
without thinking I would catch a fish.

Ellington White

Fishing brings meekness and
inspiration, reduces our egoism,
soothes our troubles
and shames our wickedness.

—

Herbert Hoover

I used to say, "I sure hope my luck changes and I catch a big fish." Then I learned that the only way for me to catch bigger fish is for ME to change.

Chuck Bauer

You've got to be ready to set the hook when the fish strikes...otherwise, you don't hook the fish.

Mark Hicks

You just never know when that next big fish is going to show up.

Bill Murphy

Why do I fish?
The easiest answer is:
My father and all my ancestors
did it before me.

—

Jimmy Carter

A crick is a distinctly separate entity from a creek.
After all, a creek is merely a creek,
but a crick is a crick.

Patrick McManus

The quicker a freshwater fish is on the fire
after he is caught, the better he is.

Mark Twain

There is a physical testing: the long hours at early
morning, in bright sun, or at dusk;
casting until your arm is like lead and your legs,
from wading against the stiff current, are numb.
That is part of the quest: to cleanse
through exertion.

Nick Lyons

There is only one theory about angling
in which I have perfect confidence,
and this is that the two words,
least appropriate to any statement, about it,
are the words "always" and "never."

Lord Edward Grey

Fishing isn't always about fishing.

Greg Milner

Fishing is a discipline
in the equality of men—
for all men are equal before fish.

—

Herbert Hoover

Part of your fishing success is about being
"on purpose" with preparation
and premeditation.

Chuck Bauer

Fishing is more fun than baseball,
watermelon and barbecues combined.

Mark Romanack

The world of angling is richly diverse.
Carp fishing with dough balls in the Charles River
is no less within its realm than the pursuit
of giant marlin off the Morro.

Nick Lyons

All Americans believe that they are born
fishermen. For a man to admit a distaste
for fishing would be like denouncing
mother-love or hating moonlight.

John Steinbeck

I can look back now and say I was born to fly cast.
While it wasn't easy, I was drawn to it.

Joan Salvato Wulff

I fish not because I regard fishing as being terribly
important, but because I suspect that
so many of the other concerns of men are equally
unimportant, and not nearly so much fun.

John Volker

Work is for those who do not fly fish.

Fisherman's Saying

O, sir, doubt not that Angling is an art;
is it not an art to deceive a trout
with an artificial fly?

Isaak Walton

The greatest angling success,
more valuable and satisfying than any trophy,
is teaching a young person to fish.

Jim Palmer

A man never stands so tall as when
he stoops to help a child fish.

Jim Porter

An old tackle box can be a gold mine
of long-forgotten treasures and a place
to find old fishing memories.

Jim Porter

The charm of fishing is that it is the pursuit of
what is elusive but attainable,
a perpetual series of occasions for hope.

John Buchan

Oh, the brave Fisher's life.
It is the best of any,
'Tis full of pleasure, void of strife,
And 'tis belov'd of many.

—

Izaak Walton

Fishing is not necessarily expensive...
though it can be.

Joe Panfalone

In truth, fishermen should do as fish do
in the summer—lie low.

Ellington White

The best time to fish is the fall.

Ellington White

Successful fishermen are curious,
drawn to a mystery, and hopeful.

Paul Quinnett

No man can be a completely good fisherman
unless within his piscatorial sphere he is generous,
sympathetic, and honest.

Grover Cleveland

If fishing is like religion,
then fly-fishing is high church.

Tom Brokaw

I still don't know why I fish
or why other men fish,
except that we like it
and it makes us think and feel.

—

Roderick Haig-Brown

It is not the fish we catch
that counts.
It is the joyous rush of the brook,
and the contemplation of
the eternal rush of the stream.

—

Herbert Hoover

Lesson 12

Timely Fishing Tips

e conclude with an assortment of suggestions about the angler's art and the fisherman's life.

My best tip:
find an expert to teach you
how to fish.

—

Dirk Mewes

In order to be a successful angler,
you must first accept
one simple fact:
There are times when fishing
is tough.

—

Roger Bacon

When, I wonder, are folks going
to learn that it is a dangerous thing
to attempt to lay down hard
and fast rules about fishing?

—

John Alden Knight

With a good partner, it doesn't seem to matter quite so much if the fish don't bite or if the ducks don't fly. His companionship can contribute more to the pleasure of your day afield than the fish you put in your creel or the game you bag.

H.G. Tapply

Plans fail when there is no counsel,
but with many advisers they succeed.
Proverbs 15:22 HCSB

Unencumbered by the knowledge that women didn't fish, it was obvious to me then, at age five or six, that it was better to be the fisherman than the rower.

Joan Salvato Wulff

The secret of successful angling depends on
learning the kind of water the fish prefer,
and then concentrating on it.

Ted Trueblood

Taking care of your fishing line is an extremely
important part of maintaining your tackle.
Change lines often.

Sam Anderson

Teamwork is reinvented in every fishing camp.

Paul Quinnett

Fisherman are advised to carry
the following essentials:
a water bottle, sunblock,
snack food, and a raincoat.

—

Dirk Mewes

Hire a guide two or three
times a year;
read fishing reports;
and talk to the experts.

—

Chuck Bauer

The fisherman who isn't plagued
with suggestions is fishing alone.

—

Beatrice Cook

I know of no fish that is improved by aging.
You can't cook a fish too soon.

Ted Trueblood

A good rod is without doubt
the angler's chief requisite.

Hardy Brothers Catalogue, 1886

As to non-members who accuse true fishermen of
falsehood, it is perfectly clear that they are utterly
unfitted to deal with the subject.

Grover Cleveland

If you need a piece of equipment,
make it as light as possible.
If you don't need it,
leave it at home.

—

Sparse Grey Hackle

When you are lucky enough
to find fish,
stay put.

—

Roger Bacon

Fish are constantly doing the most mysterious and
startling things; and no one has yet
been wise enough to explain their ways
or account for their conduct.

Grover Cleveland

Just the same, deep water off a weed bed or sand
bar, where the hungry water wolves wait for
minnows, is always a likely spot.

O. Warren Smith

What sense is there in the charge of laziness
sometimes made against true fishermen?
Laziness has no place in the constitution of
a man who starts at sunrise and tramps all day
with only a sandwich to eat, floundering through
bushes and briers and stumbling over rocks or
wading streams in pursuit of elusive trout.

Grover Cleveland

If I fished only to capture fish,
my fishing trips would have
ended long ago.

—

Zane Grey

Fishing is the eternal
Fountain of Youth.

—

Herbert Hoover